BUILDING WITH BUSES

BUILDING WITH BUSES

Daniel E. Johnson

BAKER BOOK HOUSE
Grand Rapids, Michigan

Portions of chapter 4 have been reprinted by permission from Advance by The General Council of the Assemblies of God, 1445 Boonville Ave., Springfield, Mo., 65802, Juanita Stetz, author. Also, "Building a Bus Route" is reprinted by permission of Creative Communications, Box 1578, Stow, Ohio. Lee Lebsack, author, taken from his book, THE RAVENNA MIRACLE.

Special thanks to the National Sunday School Department of the Assemblies of God for their generous help in providing information for some of the forms in this book.

Printed in the United States of America

Reprinted 1974 by
Baker Book House Company
ISBN: 0-8010-5059-6

This Book is dedicated to:

Stan Martin, our first bus captain,
Dave Johnson, our first bus driver,
Don Johnson, director of transportation;
all our able team of captains, drivers,
secretaries, and workers.

FOREWORD

Growth is a philosophical problem. Until we believe in growth, we will not strive for it. Only slightly more than half of the churches in the Northwest District of the Assemblies of God grew last year. Yet we attained the highest growth in history with an increase of 1,728 new workers. We have found most of our growth comes from the same churches each year. While God is the same in all churches, attitudes toward growth have spelled the difference.

Busing is a tremendous tool in growth. Busing requires a total commitment of the whole church to an unselfish outreach. A job half-done is often worse than a job not started. Building with buses requires a total commitment toward reaching the lost.

Harvest is not accidental. Rather, it comes to those who prepare for it. Our careful records show that busing is working everywhere. In large cities, suburban areas, small towns, and in rural areas growth is being experienced by bus-minded

Sunday schools. Busing works if done wisely and well. Dan Johnson has shown what can be done through the dynamic challenge of a bus ministry.

The contagion of Spanaway Assembly is refreshing. There is a keen sense of excitement and involvement. This did not come naturally. They have been instructed, shown what and how, and have been encouraged for what they have done. This builds great people. Like me, I am sure you will find BUILDING WITH BUSES a challenging and meaningful book about the bus ministry.

Phil Wayman, Sunday School Director
Northwest District of the
Assemblies of God

TABLE OF CONTENTS

PART I

A VITAL OUTREACH

Chapter 1

A SPIRITUAL IMPERATIVE

"How dare I stay home while the people perish?" Jim Elliot asked. This modern missionary martyr to the Indians of Ecuador captures the spiritual imperative of the believer's commission. How dare we stay home from the harvest field when men perish without Christ. And, that harvest field is not only in the remote jungles of underdeveloped nations, but at our very doorsteps.

Through evangelism in our Sunday schools we can reach those who perish in the turmoil of our times. I believe in Sunday school. Not as a department of the church; it is the church!

Dr. Oswald J. Smith, long-time pastor of People's Church in Toronto, Canada, says, "You ought to get missions out of committees and budgets and onto the platform where people can see it." The same thing applies to Sunday school. Today many Sunday schools are on the move. Declines of the 1960's and early 1970's have been reversed in hundreds of churches across our country. Large Sunday schools are proving again what can be done for God when people are interested and involved. The Sunday school is now where people can see evangelism happening and is in the forefront of a great spiritual awakening.

Large Sunday schools do not just happen. Certain principles and procedures govern Sunday school growth. From our experience we have learned growth depends on deep conviction.

Our whole Sunday school philosophy could be reduced to three simple statements:

(1) SIN IS WHAT GOD SAYS IT IS

Henrietta Mears observed, "No man is great who has not wept over sin." If we reach the lost we must be moved by the tragedy sin brings to our land and people. There is no other way to be effective. Unless our hearts are broken by the heartbreak of our world, we will not be moved to help heal the hurt of those about us.

What is sin? It is divorce; a little girl standing in the rain waiting for a daddy who will never come back. It is crime and corruption; a crying mother seeing her son being rudely pushed into a filthy jail cell. It is sickness; a dying child crippled by a dread disease of another's sin. We play down emotions. "Don't get too excited," we say. Yet we must get excited if we heal our dying world. I think we ought to get upset and angry at sin. Jesus was "troubled in spirit," and "wept over Jerusalem." He often "sighed" in His spirit and had His grueling "Gethsemane." Often His soul was deeply troubled. Sin is real and is tragic.

(2) GOD'S WORD MAKES A DIFFERENCE

As a stone crashing down the mountain smites the image, so the Bible deals with sin. We are not helpless twigs in the stream of time. We can change our world by bringing the healing power of Christ to our nations and neighborhoods. While sin takes a tragic toll, "He sent his word, and healed them, and delivered them from their destructions." (Psalms 107:20). The Sunday school reaches the lost and teaches the TRUTH.

(3) GOD HAS CALLED US

The world lies bleeding and ravaged by sin. But, there is total healing through Christ. God has called us to bring the therapy of God's Word to the wounded of our world. Each of our Sunday school workers is deeply impressed with his clear-cut calling. They are assigned to their tasks by the Great Physician, not merely a harried departmental superintendent or a busy pastor. Like Jeremiah they seem to hear God say, "Before I formed thee in the belly I knew thee; and before thou camest forth out of the womb I sanctified thee, and I ordained thee a prophet unto the nations." (Jeremiah 1:5)

BASIC SUNDAY SCHOOL PRINCIPLES

When Robert Raikes started the Sunday school movement he based his approach on four specific principles. Although Sunday school has come of age, his basic principles still form the core of a viable program.

(1) LAYMEN WILL TEACH

Mr. Raikes insisted laymen were to teach. While the paid clergy played an important part in the Sunday school movement, the "common" Christian was charged with the responsibility of Sunday school teaching. Today the Sunday school is still a layman's movement, and must remain so. Many churches are adding paid staff to teach and coordinate. While this at times is necessary, I feel it might be a dangerous trend. The laymen must be involved if great growth is achieved.

(2) GOD'S WORD TAUGHT

Of utmost importance was curriculum. Mr. Raikes was careful to make sure the Bible, not catechism, formed the curriculum of his Sunday school. Today we have many teaching aids and tools. However, the Bible must still be the basis of all our teaching. Care must be taken that materials used exalt Christ and are thoroughly Bible based. Many of the children we bring on buses will have no additional opportunities to learn about the Bible. Thus, our mission is doubly important. We must inform and inspire so an insatiable hunger of heart will be developed in them that nothing else can fill.

(3) OPEN TO ALL

All children were to be reached. Effective Sunday schools reach not just the children of the church families, but all children of the community. Some ask, "What will busing do to our morning service?" In answer, it is something similar to what six new babies would do to your home. Like babies, busing demands expansion, understanding, and patience. However, the benefits are well worth the trouble. We must reach all children, not just those in our church. The challenge of Sunday school has always been clear.

(4) EVANGELISM FIRST

The one thrust was evangelism. "Education is important," Mr. Raikes noted, "but evangelism is the priority." This is why we put up with crowding and inconvenience. We strive for quality Christian education, but reaching the lost is our primary goal. Really, the two cannot be separated. If we reach people, we must be prepared to teach and take care of them.

It would be well to remember the church in Jerusalem had no building, no budget, no buses, no blackboards, or overhead projectors. Yet, they reached thousands of people with the Gospel of Christ. Winning the lost was their priority. I like the word "soul-winning." This word is better than "witnessing," "saying a word for Jesus," or "sharing Christ." Evangelism is our thrust and we are winning souls for the Lord we love.

TWO SUNDAY SCHOOLS

Three years ago I accepted the pastorate of Spanaway Assembly with an average Sunday school attendance of 182. After reading the records, viewing the situation, and comparing our church with others in our area, I concluded we ought to grow. If we could just increase 25 people a year. I thought that would be substantial growth. Many of our area churches were declining and only a few were registering sizeable gains.

Not long after my decision a friend came to see me. I showed him around and told him my goals, "We're going to add an average of 25 this year. If we can do that each year for five years, we will become a strong church." I waited for his approval nudging him with, "That would be pretty good growth, wouldn't it?"

"Pretty good," he agreed, not enthusiastically.

I pressed him, "You can't expect to grow much faster than that can you?"

"That's up to you," he said, and left me to ponder my plight.

I began to think. Why couldn't we grow more than 25 annually? My friend, by refusing to approve my plans, had provoked me to making a great discovery. I concluded that too often we limit ourselves. In our first year we grew 51 in attendance. The second year we increased by 175. This past year we gained 208 and as this book is going to press we are averaging 300 to 400 more than a year ago.

VISION! A viable vision is what we need. We limit ourselves! Napoleon Hill noted, "Man can create anything he can imagine." One is not likely to achieve anything he cannot see.

Every good pastor, Sunday school superintendent, and teacher has two Sunday schools. The first exists on each Sunday morning and the other lives in his heart. Both are very real. He lives with the first and works toward the second. He is motivated to build because the secret of motivation is vision. Thoughts determine what we have and where we go. A very wise man observed, "Men who see the invisible, hear the inaudible, believe the incredible, think the unthinkable, are the men who do the impossible."

Dr. Elmer Towns stirred my heart deeply when he said, "Sunday schools have grown in direct proportion to the determination of teachers reflecting the conviction that boys and girls and men and women must be reached with the message of the Bible, or be lost forever." Thus, Sunday schools must grow. Dr. W. A. Criswell quipped, "There's nothing wrong with a small Sunday school, but there's something wrong with a Sunday school that is not growing." John R. Rice said, "There's nothing wrong with a small Sunday school–for about six months."

A viable vision makes patience possible. The sage observed, "He who has patience can have what he will." If we can visualize the church God wants us to build, then we can endure all to build it. We can put up with criticism, opposition, failure, disappointment, and the devil himself, because we see what God wants us to do. God has involved us in this exciting building process. We, too, can do the impossible as we are locked in to our deep commitment to Christ and settled in our vision for the lost.

God's Word claims, "The secret of the Lord is with them that fear him; and he will shew them his covenant." (Psalms 25:14). Each can catch that heavenly vision and make his life count for Christ. At times God calls us from the "madding crowd" to share these secrets with us.

Recently, my little boy was about to be scolded in front of the family. His face turned white and he rushed to me whispering, "Can we talk about it somewhere else?" "Sure," I said So we had a private meeting in the bedroom. God does that for us. He affords us those private times when we settle things. Today may God call us aside to stir us with the challenge of the lost.

We have a divine imperative to win the lost. Sunday schools provide the most logical platform for preaching Christ. And, we have found a fantastic surge in our Sunday school since we have started to build with buses.

Chapter 2

DOES THE BUS MINISTRY PAY?

On a recent Sunday morning one of our fourth grade teachers was recognizing visitors when a little boy stood up to give his name. The small lad started to cry and after gentle probing the teacher discovered his home was breaking up. The boy's heart was broken and the divorce would shatter his life for years to come. He clutched his gift Bible in desperation feeling at least he could hold onto something. This child was brought to Sunday school on our buses. These are the kinds of people we reach through our bus ministry.

In recruiting personnel for our bus routes I often say, "If you will go visiting two Saturdays and ride on a bus three Sundays, you will be hooked." When you see the sorrow and sadness of so many, it gets hold of you. I never go visiting on our bus routes without coming home wishing all I had to do would be to knock on doors and bring people to Sunday school.

One Sunday afternoon I rode home with the bus children. I did not realize how far our buses went and before we finished it was 2:45 p.m. and my dinner was cold. The bus captain on that route, Gary Trauter, also covers two other routes with three buses. He has some of our church ladies to bake cakes for the children when someone has a birthday. Sometimes they serve 200 cupcakes with Scripture verses in pink icing.

This Sunday I went along the boys and girls bounced on the bus asking for cupcakes. As they ate their treats, I saw how much they enjoyed this time and wondered if these pastries were the nicest things some of them had eaten in a week.

The first home I visited when we began our bus ministry was that of Dick and Judy Phillips. God ordained that our first contact was productive. The next morning we picked up the five Phillips children and Sunday evening the parents came, bringing back their children. All were saved and became members of our church. As an unemployed bartender Dick Phillips was posed with the problem of finding work. Soon he got a good job and their family life drastically changed. I shall never forget his testimony a few months later, He said they were happier, had more material possessions and since they were saved their marriage had been like a honeymoon. People like the Phillips who have been changed by the power of Christ convince me the bus ministry pays.

IT PAYS IN NUMBERS GAINED

Without apology I say we are interested in numbers. When someone says he is not interested in numbers, I think something is wrong. If on payday you receive your salary and find it is short, you suddenly are interested in numbers. When you go to the grocery store to buy five dollars worth of groceries and you give the checker a twenty dollar bill, if he returns only three dollars change, you are interested in numbers. If suddenly you have 15 teeth instead of 32, you would be very interested in numbers. Far more important than salary, money, or teeth, is the eternal soul of a man. Therefore, we are interested in numbers.

It seems strange that a slowly declining church is seldom criticized, but when a church starts to reach large numbers of people, criticism comes. Perhaps the most frequent comment of criticism against such a surging church is, "It is not stable growth." It should be remembered the church of Acts had 3,000 converted in a single day. Yet, they seemed to have little trouble in stabilizing their assembly. We are interested in reaching the largest number of people we possibly can for Jesus Christ.

Some say a little church serves the people better than a larger one. They claim the people are more actively involved in smaller congregations. Slogans have been coined to express this thought, "A church small enough to know you, yet large enough to serve you." This is fuzzy thinking. If we really believe the Bible, we must try to reach the greatest number of people possible. A viable bus ministry is one of the most powerful means to reach a community for Christ. Numbers are people and we are interested in numbers.

The single most important factor contributing to church growth is commitment to growth. If we have a deep drive to grow, we will. People are lost without Christ and we must reach them. If it is right to reach five, then it is right to reach 20. If it's right to reach 20, then why not 50? And, if it is right to reach 50, why not reach 100? Dr. Elmer Towns emphasizes that our Sunday schools grow in direct proportion to the desire of teachers and leaders. I feel we have no choice but to try our best to reach the largest numbers of people possible. It is really not right for us to be academic about the problem of size when people around us are without Jesus Christ.

Numbers are people! A little girl sat in my wife's Sunday school class recently. The lead teacher was talking about Christ being crucified for our sins. The little girl listened and then tapped my wife's arm asking, "Is that really true?" My wife assured her the story was true and the girl replied, "I've never heard that before." She is a number.

Not long ago a teenage girl came to our church for the first time and gave her heart to the Lord. A few weeks later she suddenly became ill and within two days was dead. Tina was a number. We also had a negative experience that reemphasized the importance of numbers to us. Steve came to our church on Easter Sunday. Tragically, we never got around to visit him at his home. Although he came to church that once, he never gave his heart to the Lord. Not long after Easter he and his sister got into a violent argument. He stormed out of the house, jumped into his car and roared down a steep hill. Another car was coming up the incline and Steve could not control his veering vehicle. He died instantly in the crash. Seventeen-year-old Steve was a number.

We must look at numbers as people. How can we academically argue about the Sunday school numbers game? We are not talking about statistics; we are talking about lost and lonely people. I walked through our children's church service the other day when John, a young black, stopped me. John was a known trouble-maker for the teachers and he confronted me with, "You're Pastor Johnson, aren't you?" After I assured him I was he commanded, "Sit down here." We sat listening to the teachers for a few minutes. John sprawled his foot over the chair in front of him.

A little girl turned around and said in a child-like manner, "My dog died." John replied, "My dad died." When I probed deeper I found John's dad had just died in jail. John is a number. Busing provides a way to reach the Tinas, Steves, and Johns. Each Sunday we bring 400 children and teenagers to our church on buses. I make no apology for this high ratio of bus people to regular church members. We are in the business of reaching people for Christ. Buses will build numbers. However, we must remember our motivation. We are increasing our numbers, not for a sense of self-satisfaction, but because each number is a person for whom Christ died.

BUSES PAY IN SOULS SAVED

How shall they hear without a preacher? People cannot be saved unless they hear the Word of God. Without doubt some of the greatest people in the world are Sunday school teachers. They implant God's Word in human hearts. God's Word is powerful. It has eternity in it. When we put the Scripture in the human mind and heart, we have planted something there that will never die.

The dramatic story of Dawson Trotman proves the power of the Word. Trotman was a teenage rebel. He met a pretty girl and found she went to church. He, wanting to impress her, attended the youth meeting. The youth group was having a contest memorizing Bible verses. Dawson decided to see if he could do it. He memorized ten verses. On the next week he memorized another ten. Still unconverted and living a rebelious life, Dawson got drunk and was thrown in jail. Later he was released and on Monday morning began to walk to work. Suddenly the Holy Spirit began bringing the Scriptures he had memorized to his mind. Dawson stopped, found a Bible and on that way to work, gave his heart to the Lord. His life eternally changed through the power of the Word.

Time after time we have seen the Word grip our bus children. When we bring them to our Sunday school and they hear the Word they are arrested by it. Sometimes outward appearance is deceiving. Yet, even though it doesn't seem like they are listening, one by one we see them give their hearts to Christ.

Not long ago a group of teenagers began riding our bus each week. They would create havoc for our driver, but he tolerated them. The gang was rowdy and one girl among them was one of the most arrogant and insolent persons I have ever met. Whenever we had a youth party she would always spoil it with her horrible attitude. She had no manners and delighted in being obnoxious. One Sunday I rode the bus with the teenagers and noticed the girl had completely changed. She was kind and sweet and actually acted like a human being. When she got off the bus I asked the driver why the difference. He replied, "She got saved today." Relaying the story to me, the driver said the girl's name was Alice. "A couple of Sundays ago," he said, "we brought in some young people for church. Alice just stood outside when we encouraged them to go into Sunday school. She said she didn't have to come here and no one was going to boss her around. I was firm with her and finally she went in. Today, she came up after Sunday school to have me sign the Bible they gave her announcing, "I got saved this morning." This is the best way to solve discipline problems, by getting them saved in our Sunday schools.

We bring people on buses so they might hear the eternal Word of God. I am convinced as they have this Word planted in their hearts God's Holy Spirit will call it to their attention and they will find Christ as personal Savior. These bus children will not be moved by our brilliant programs or offers of hospitality. These things are necessary and nice. But, it is the Word of God taught and preached that reaches them and changes their lives.

Busing pays in souls saved. As we go out into the communities with an evangelistic thrust, we will reap the benefits of those labors. We are careful to communicate to all our bus workers that the whole purpose of our program is to teach God's Word and thus reach pupils' hearts for the Lord. If you still doubt that busing pays, I challenge you to try it. With an evangelistic thrust in your bus ministry, you can and will see more souls saved than you even thought possible.

BUSING PAYS IN FAMILIES REACHED

Busing reaches whole families. When we first started our bus ministry we went to the Mayfair section of our city. Ten of our workers knocked on every door in the entire area and only got riders out of two houses. One of the families we met that day was the Fryers. They promised to let their two sons attend our church. Each week Mike and Steve came home telling their folks what they had learned in Sunday school and church. They even took cassette recordings home and played them for Sunday dinner.

Several months went by as God continued to deal with the parents. Their personal problems mounted. In the small hours of a Saturday morning, they returned from one of their parties. Their whole lives seemed empty and together they prayed God would send someone to talk to them. That very morning our bus workers visited their home. For over an hour they talked with the Fryers about Christ and at the end of that time Steve and Cheri Fryer knelt in their front room to give their lives to Christ. Today, they are active members of our church and attend every Sunday.

Through the Fryers we have gained many more families. We are continually reaching whole family units through our buses. About a year ago a lady and her four children moved within a few blocks of our church. She had come down to our area from Seattle to be close to her husband who was an inmate of McNeil Island prison. Her very first week in town she was visited by our bus workers. We picked her and the children up for church the next morning. She and all her children were saved that day. On her next visit to McNeil Island she told her husband what had happened. He gave his heart to Christ. The story does not end there. A sister-in-law was having marital trouble. Through the testimony of the newly converted couple she was saved and their marriage survived. Later the husband was released from prison and comes to our church. The other day we were trying to raise money for a new bus and I noticed he was one of the first to make a contribution. He also works on our buses to keep them running.

Occasionally someone will ask, "Do you ever reach any adults on your bus routes?" Even if we never reached any adults, we would still bus people in. What is wrong with reaching children?

However, we do reach many adults. We have 175 teenagers in our Sunday school every week with many riding our buses. In a few years they will get married and become the adult section of our church. As the previous testimonies have indicated, we have won whole families through interest in their children.

One of the best ways to reach parents is to make contacts each week in the bus ministry. We attempt to reach parents in three ways. (1) We sow the Gospel seed. Each time we visit the seed is watered with our interest. At some time everyone needs a church. When they are sick or if they learn they have a terminal disease or when tragedy comes, they have a deep need for the comfort of a church. We have planted the seed and they seek us out in their trouble. Hundreds of people in our city look to us as their church home. I have never seen some of them, but they call us. Every week someone contacts us to visit a neighbor or friend in the hospital. These calls result from our bus ministry. At the hospital I get to know parents. At times these come to our church. (2) Children will reach their parents. Through personal witness and persistence parents are touched by our church through their children. Many parents have come into our assembly through this means. (3) We carefully explain a child's conversion to his parent. We go to parents and tell them what God has done in the lives of their children. We ask parents' permission for water baptism and suggest they come when this takes place. Through this means we have opportunity to discuss spiritual values with whole families.

We also have many adults who ride our buses. Recently we baptized a couple in their middle fifties who came to the Lord in our church. They ride to our church each week on our buses.

We have found buses open the door to witnessing. Our gospel team and Sunday school teachers have ready access into hundreds of homes because they care for the children. Hardly ever is a door slammed in our face because the children know who we are.

BUSING PAYS IN MONEY GIVEN

This may sound strange since busing does not pay its own way. Yet, the first year we engaged in the bus ministry we nearly doubled our income. God sent in the money. God is no man's debtor. The Bible has much to say about consideration and ministry to the poor and the needy. We found when we sacrificed in this ministry, God blessed abundantly.

God is never behind in paying His debts. I remember several months ago a man called me on the phone to say he was going into the hospital the next day and insisted on seeing me.

I did not know the man, but discovered later that he had grandchildren from two different families, riding our buses. Doctors discovered he had cancer and was given only a few weeks to live. Before he died we led him to Christ. Before his death his home was reconciled. In appreciation he made several large donations to our building fund and bus ministry. His son and wife were also saved and are now part of our regular church family.

One man sent in a sizeable check and he had never been to our church. He still does not come and is not even a Christian. However, he saw what the church is doing and was impressed. He felt our assembly deserved his support. The world is impressed by a church that cares for people.

Someone once asked me if we had black people riding our buses. Up to that moment the thought had not even occurred to me. We are interested in reaching souls, black people, white people, oriental people, rich people, and poor people. Yes, we have blacks. We have all people of our city. Our churches should represent our communities. We do not have racial problems in our assembly. God pity the church that decides to close its doors to anyone in its community. One pastor confessed, "I've got the finest Sunday morning service and everything is going smooth. I'm thinking about busing, but I don't know what it will do to my service." Pity that pastor. Our churches must be soul-winning stations for the lost, not private clubs for some segments of our society. The church must be a place where all people can come. Let the poor come, the rich, the high, and the low. All can be saved by the power of the Holy Spirit.

A church that opens its arms to all peoples will find God providing the needed money. When skeptics ask, "What class of people do you have in your church?" I reply, "They are all first class." When we take care of the poor, God takes care of us.

BUSING PAYS IN PEOPLE DEVELOPED

The first step in recruiting personnel is creating the need for people. Some might ask, "Do you get all the workers you need?" In answer, we are never satisfied. You never have what you need, but you just keep creating the need asking God to help you. We have a Sunday school session at 9:45 a.m. and another at 11 a.m. We had to bring in more workers. We have many people in our church who never eat Sunday dinner before 3 p.m. We have found these dedicated people develop great spiritual insight and have an intense relationship with the Lord.

When one helps and loves people he grows in grace. These are not the ones who criticize or create problems for the pastoral staff. Active workers in the kingdom are mature people who find satisfaction by working for the Lord. Doug Greesey is an example of how people develop when they are sold out to God.

Doug began helping Carl Philliber in the bus ministry. When Carl went to Bible school, Doug took over the route with two buses. He works faithfully each week spending three or four hours on Saturday visiting. He gets up early on Sunday, gets home late for Sunday dinner, and while other youth are playing on Sunday afternoon, he's taking care of his bus route. He is back in church on Sunday night and Wednesday night. What a thrill to see how spiritually healthy this young man is. If we never reached anybody, just to see all these people who are involved in the work of God would be worth it.

If we run a little holding operation with everything under tight control, we will never know the thrill of seeing people develop through spiritual labor.

When I accepted our church pastorate Stan Martin was not living for the Lord. I will remember forever when at an altar service he took my arm and asked me to pray for him. He was gloriously saved and became our first bus captain. Later he asked to start a bus ministry and from that has grown our outreach. Through this work Stan has grown into a strong Christian.

People in our church feel called to do what

they do, just as much as I feel called to be the pastor. They have grown in their God-called-tasks. Many people who are involved in our bus ministry have been reached through buses. One of our Sunday school superintendents was raised in an ungodly home and living in sin. Somebody came by her house one day with a Sunday school bus and brought her to our Sunday school. She found the Lord and soon had a desire to work for Him. She has developed our third and fourth grade departments with over a hundred in attendance. She came in through our bus outreach and grew in the Lord.

God said let there be light. The devil would blind the minds of our world. I believe the day for the church is now. This is the time right now when we have the dollars, the personnel, the methods. We have things the early church did not have to reach people. What we need now is to have our hearts stirred and burned. Jesus Christ is coming soon and we want to reach large numbers of people. We are not satisfied with the status quo. We want to reach all men for Christ. We are interested in numbers because numbers are people. We want to see new income in our church to increase and we want to see our people trained and motivated. You too share that same desire and I challenge you to try reaching the people around you through building with buses.

Chapter 3

WHAT OTHERS ARE SAYING ABOUT THE BUS MINISTRY

Five years ago most Christian educators predicted buses were on the way out. Some pastors even sold the buses they had and started other programs to reach their communities. Sadly, they have found that they threw out the baby with the bathwater. Buses do something for a church that no other evangelistic effort can. Therefore, many of these same pastors are now buying back buses and are becoming involved once more in reaching their town with buses.

In recent months many articles have been written about the bus ministry. All over our country pastors are considering an active bus ministry. Recently, Juanita Stetz interviewed three prominent pastors and found them excited about building with buses. She reported the following:

Busing people to church has become increasingly popular. Perhaps you've considered extending your church's outreach in this manner. To help you decide, we interviewed three pastors whose churches are now operating buses.

William Douglas, Christian Assembly, Zion, Illinois, is the pastor of a long-established, but recently rapid-growing church which operates seven buses and two vans.

Darwin Heuser is pastor of Calvary Temple in Waukegan, Illinois, a growing church averaging over 500 last year.

John Thompson has been pastor of First Assembly in Kenosha, Wisconsin, for less than a year. This is a long-established church with a Sunday school averaging over 500. He has had considerable experience with church busing in his previous pastorate in Kansas City, Missouri, as well. The Waukegan and Zion churches launched their bus ministries less than two years ago.

Here are highlights of the interviews:

What has the bus ministry done for your churches?

Heuser: It has helped our attendance.

Thompson: The bus ministry has given a greater opportunity for evangelism.

Douglas: We have had a decided increase in the number of souls saved. As many as 350 souls were saved during 1973. This hasn't all been a result of the bus ministry, but it has played a large part.

Then you would say the bus ministry has increased your outreach?

Douglas: Very much so. Not just children, but we reach far more families than ever before. Last Saturday one of our bus workers was making the rounds of her route. In one of the homes, she came across a woman who seemed to have quite a need. At the worker's suggestion the woman called me. When I got there, I felt the only answer was God, so it was an easy task to lead her to the Lord.

Don't you think this creates more enthusiasm among your own people as they see others coming and realize they are a part of it all?

Douglas: I think it has revitalized our church and its outlook. Of course, it can have a reverse effect in some instances when you have such a large element from unchurched homes.

Heuser: Last March when we averaged 623, a couple of families put up some objections. Since our space is limited, they felt we were more concerned with ministering to outsiders than to our own church kids.

Can you give some concrete examples of homes or individuals influenced for Christ as a direct result of this outreach?

Douglas: I had a baptismal service last October for five persons, all of whom came in through the bus ministry. In November, 21 adults and young people were baptized. These were bus ministry people.

Thompson: Just before I came to this church they had a number of junior and teen boys saved and filled with the Spirit—as many as seven in one night.

Heuser: I can think of one family who recently made a commitment to the Lord as a result of the bus ministry.

What type of people do you reach with your buses?

Heuser: Most of those we have reached are the more transient type. They are from the unchurched lower to middle class.

Thompson: We reach basically those in areas with substandard housing.

Douglas: Some question whether bus ministry is worthwhile because of the type of people you reach. But we feel these people need the gospel. We have Spanish and blacks along with the whites. I find coming to Sunday school has transformed their attitude toward the house of God.

How do you sustain children's interest in Sunday school when their parents do not attend?

Douglas: First of all, we try to have a Sunday school session that will appeal. The hour wasn't long enough, so now from the junior department down we continue Sunday school through the worship service hour. We have a half-hour lesson, songs, memory work, a short recess, handcraft, and many things correlated into the teaching program.

Thompson: We try to maintain interest through visitation. The bus pastors call, and the teachers visit also. We offer little prizes. Then we show them love. That is probably the ingredient lacking in their homes.

Douglas: One thing I'd like to mention that is significant: While we have been growing with the bus program, we also have more people coming on their own than ever before.

To be altogether objective about this, what would you give as some disadvantages to this type of outreach?

Douglas: We tend to get some static from the

parents and children who come on their own because we are always doing things for the bus people, such as giving them breakfast, passing out candy, etc. That's a drawback. We try to compensate by doing something for the others at times.

We have problems with facilities because we are growing so rapidly. We don't have enough workers. We are always working with an element of youngsters who haven't been to church much before. They have to be taught how to behave. That creates bigger discipline problems.

Heuser: The way I see it, when we get more than one-fourth to one-third of the kids who've been unchurched, it brings problems. When the ratio gets too great, it envelops our own church kids, and they are influenced.

How would you summarize the bus outreach? Is it an asset or a burden to your church?

Thompson: It's a ministry of the church. It's endeavoring to take the gospel to everyone.

Pastor Lee Lebsack of one of America's fastest growing churches recently wrote a book outlining their phenomenal growth. So important is the bus ministry to their work that he included one whole chapter about his bus ministry. Here is what he said:

Busing is not new. Not long ago, I read one of D. L. Moody's books. Back in 1886, Dr. Moody said, "In these country towns, the difficulty is people have so far to go that if they have no conveyance, they think they must stay at home. A plan was suggested that we get some wagons, and you will see them around here now. One was called 'Church Wagon No. 1,' and another 'Church Wagon No. 2.'

"We arranged to have farmers hitch their horses to these wagons. Some people have no horses and just bring 16 non-church goers in each of those wagons. We have one wagon at this end of town and the other at the other end."

Praise the Lord for men of vision like D. L. Moody.

Busing is more than transportation; it is soul winning. It must be a personal interest ministry. To be really effective, we must systematically try to win parents of those who ride our buses. To help us do this, every Monday night we have a soul-winning night. Here, our people meet, have prayer, and then are assigned to go out and win souls on our bus routes. Getting into the homes is easy because their children come to our church. In our bus ministry, our goal is to win every parent to the Lord and encourage him to drive his children to Sunday school.

At Ravenna, we have definite days when we honor parents of bus children. The child receives a prize if the parents attend with the child on that day. Often, we take a survey to determine what members of each bus family do not attend our Sunday school. We have found grandparents, brothers and sisters along with parents who do not attend our Sunday school, but live in the same house. These are extra prospects for salvation and can be won to Christ and be brought into church life.

A church's attitude toward bus children is vital. We must be careful not to alienate the bus children from others in our church. We discovered, much to our sadness, that some people differentiate between "our" children and "bus" children. And, most children are very sensitive and can immediately detect this attitude. We are constantly alert to this problem and seek to make certain all children in our Sunday school are treated the same. Therefore, we do not separate them from other classes or have them seated in any one particular part of the church. Adults have learned these children need to be helped in learning reverence and help them in a careful and loving way. We have taught our people to be responsible. They become the children's parents while they are in church.

Every church should strive to make the bus ministry a vital part of the outreach. Prayer groups for this ministry should be set up, and it must be considered a real missionary effort of the church. The bus ministry is never just an attendance getter. Rather, it is an arm used to win people and change lives. When one goes into the bus ministry, he will be criticized. While perhaps some have abused this powerful soul-winning tool, let us not throw out the baby with the bath water. With proper motivation and planning, the bus ministry can be a powerful evangelistic effort.

When I first came to Ravenna, the church had one bus which brought in 10 children each Sunday. At that time, I knew nothing of how to build a bus route and could find no magazines or books to help me. But, we knew something had to be done. All I could think of was to go out every Saturday and knock on doors to try to build a route. Soon, we had 35 on the bus each week, and we added another bus. Today, we have many buses and have developed an excellent workable system for building a bus ministry. While the plan is not original with us, it is helping build hundreds of Sunday schools across America who reach thousands for Christ.

Each bus on our routes has a captain. The captain is preferably not the driver. At the beginning, we had a shortage of helpers and had to combine the jobs. However, this is not the ideal situation. The bus captain is responsible for attendance on the bus. He is required to visit a minimum of three hours each week plus get 10 new promises of attendance. During the three hours of visitation, he calls on the bus families reminding them that he will be by Sunday morning. Regardless of whether the family was absent or present the Sunday before, he must call on them. This is urgent because many of these families show little interest in the children going to Sunday school. When the captain drops by every Saturday, they come to realize how important it is to you for their children to attend.

Captains are the key to a successful route. We set a goal to average 40 riders on each route. Many of our captains have more than 40 and continue to pack their buses. Sometimes we have as many as 100 riding a bus for a special Sunday.

Another key in building a route is for the pastor to show an intense interest in the bus ministry. I meet with our captains every Sunday to go over reports with them and to encourage them in their ministry. When the captains come in on Sunday, they fill out a report telling how many hours they visited, how many people were on their buses, and how many new promises of attendance they had. We carefully file these cards so we know how well each captain is progressing. In these meetings, we set goals for each captain for the following week.

Although the pastor maintains close weekly contact, direct supervision is given to our head bus captain. He is on our staff full time and handles any problems the bus captains have.

He is in charge of emergency replacements for both captain and driver. He also helps recruit new captains and drivers.

In addition to our bus captains, we found it extremely helpful to have a special visitation task force go out twice a week soliciting riders for the buses. These people are called our "door knockers" and spend two hours each Tuesday and Thursday in visitation. They usually call on 200 to 600 people per week building the bus routes. Prospects they get each week are turned over to the head bus captain who passes them to individual bus captains. He will then go out and make a Saturday visit on these people.

GETTING WORKERS

The most frequent question asked by interested pastors is, "How do you get workers?" We look for those who love kids. We have found ladies make excellent bus captains. We make appeals from the pulpit and in every opportunity talk up the bus ministry. I preach messages on soul winning and zero in with the fact of the greatest areas of soul winning is in the bus ministry. One family in our church took one of our buses and, within a few months built a route from seven to more than 40 every Sunday.

Another aid in recruiting helpers is when we feature bus captains who give their testimony in the Sunday night services showing what is happening in the bus ministry. This encourages others to work in this important ministry.

BUS ROUTE PROMOTION

On our buses, we use a completely different approach in promotion. In the bus program, we utilize a "give-away" system for motivation. In other areas of our Sunday school, there are few contests and "give-aways." But, with the bus ministry, it is completely different. Here, we are working in a different area with non-church people, and our approach must be different. We have special days for our bus riders. On some days, we give hamburgers and cokes to all kids who ride. We have "kite" Sunday, a Dairy Queen Sunday, and even a "Case of Pepsi" day. Everyone who brings the most visitors on each bus gets a case of Pepsi. We also have a penny jar where everyone who brings the most can reach in the penny jar and get as many pennies his hand will hold. On Thanksgiving weekend, we have a "turkey" Sunday where the one who brings the most visitors on each bus gets a turkey. We have "yoyo" Sunday and everyone receives a yoyo. There is no limit to what can be done on a bus route to assure attendance.

It is important to remember that the ultimate goal of every teacher and captain is to win that boy or girl for Christ. Each Sunday, our teachers give altar calls in the classrooms. Then, the teacher hands in a report to the Sunday school office of how many were saved that day. Bus captains receive this report so they know how many have found Christ from their bus each week. He then will talk to the child about his new experience and tries to help him grow in the Lord. The teacher is also required to follow-up on this conversion to make certain we have done all we can to help that child and family.

FINANCING THE BUS MINISTRY

Some ask how to finance the bus ministry. First, it is important we sell our people on the bus work as a soul winning ministry. Then, there are some suggested ways to help pay for it. We use the general budget of the church with special offerings taken once a quarter. Sometimes, our Wednesday night offerings are used for this work. We have found as long as we keep the bus ministry before the people, monies come in. A final word on how to buy a bus.

Some churches may feel it is impractical or that they are too small for such an investment. However, a Sunday school bus is not expensive in purchase or operation if handled correctly. The initial cost of a bus is not the only thing to consider seriously. Licenses, insurance, operating expenses, maintenance, and storage will make up a large portion of a bus' cost. We discussed these expenses and investigated to find out exactly how much it would cost us annually to operate our bus. After these figures were obtained, a report was brought to the committee and a financial plan was set up.

One capable mechanic outlined what he felt was important in looking for a bus. He first checked all the bus seats for tears or holes. Next, he looked closely at the bus body for rust spots and to see if it was fairly airtight with the doors sealing well when closed. A good heater was important because of the cold northern winters. And, he looked for the latest in bus body styles since we would keep the bus for years and wanted it to look as new as possible.

Why did he look first at these items rather than the motor or transmission? The mechanic explained, "These things cannot be repaired inexpensively."

Next came the motor. He checked to see if the oil pressure remained stable while driving, especially after the motor became warm. He listened carefully to the sound of the engine and checked it as much as possible. The transmission and differential were next in line. If these were not good, he would hear a high-pitched hum raise and lower like the sound of snow tires on dry pavement.

Surprisingly, he placed little emphasis on the

tires. He stated that on a Sunday school bus, the tires rot out before they wear out. However, he did check the sidewalls to see if they could be recapped. A Sunday school bus is driven less than one fifth the miles a regular school bus travels, he explained and it is far more important to get a good solid body, good seats, and interior than to worry about the tires. A bus depreciates more from standing still than running. He also looked for a large body because a large bus is no more expensive to operate than a small one and is much more comfortable and convenient.

Most state laws require a church bus must be painted a different color than a regular school bus. You will also want professional lettering on the bus.

A bus is a tremendous blessing to the Sunday school and church. We continue to reach new families for Christ through the bus route, and our Sunday school benefits both numerically as well as financially. Also, it has drawn our people closer together since we have more times of fellowship and go together as a unit. In addition to Sunday school and vacation Bible school, we have used our bus for camps, retreats, scouting trips, outings, picnics, rallies, fellowship meetings, and church dedications.

We encourage all to get a bus.

Chapter 4

COMMON QUESTIONS ASKED ABOUT THE BUS MINISTRY

Each year we have a "bus anniversary." On this day we officially recognize the ministry of this outreach and encourage our people to get involved. It is always one of the biggest days of the year. Because of the dramatic growth of our church through busing, many write asking questions to help them get started.

We began with 13 riders on a 38-passenger bus. Today we run seven buses with 12 routes. On a given Sunday we will bring in over 500. There is no quicker or cheaper way to reach large numbers of people than through busing. Two of our college girls bring over 80 people each week. This is as many people as some churches have.

(1) Is busing for every church?

Each church leader must carefully consider all that is involved before going into busing. I suggest that each examines the philosophy and program of the church to see if people are ready for busing. Busing will change the character, shape, and size of the church. It will affect everything done, the format of the services, and thinking of the leadership. Why do you want to reach people? Is it just to keep up with other churches or is it that busing is now popular? Is the church really committed to growth?

A church must be moving before getting into busing. You must have personnel to recruit other personnel who can get the job done. Busing is hard work. You reach all kinds of people, every culture, color, and background. Unless one really believes in busing it is a mistake to get into it. The bus ministry must be understood as a tool of evangelism and supported wholeheartedly by the entire church.

(2) Do parents complain when they are visited every Saturday?

No. There may be an exception, but we have had no problem. The bus captain merely appears at the door for 20 or 30 seconds to make sure they are coming the following day. In many cases the parents do not care whether the kids go. Sometimes the parents say, "Well, we'll wake them up if they want to go." It is up to our bus captain to keep a good rapport between the children and himself.

(3) Should a Pastor head the bus program?

Definitely yes! However, it is very important to get bus workers recruiting other workers. We give points to our workers to recruit. These points count on their monthly evaluation sheets. Whoever runs the bus program still has to have the pastor heavily involved or it will never go. It is not an off-shoot of the church, it involves the whole church.

(4) How do you handle the influx of people?

We have to take care of these people and be willing to make whatever changes necessary. It is just like a family with a new baby, adjustments must be made to accomodate the new arrival. Tragically, some people in churches are not willing to make room for new people. Some have been critical of our program saying, "You can't take care of all those people and run a good church program." My answer is that we are constantly making necessary changes. We continue to enlarge rooms, change our program, and make innovations. Growing always involves adjustments.

(5) How do you finance the bus ministry?

There are many ways. Some do it through the missions program. While we never take away from our foreign and home missionaries, I emphasize the bus outreach every Sunday morning in my adult class. Thus, people are always giving money for buses. Some of our congregation have bought buses and given them to us. We have had people borrow money to buy a bus for the church.

(6) How does your bus routing work?

We have two bus crews. When the first buses get in at 9:30 a.m., a second bus captain, driver, and secretary goes out to bring in another group. We have a second Sunday school session at 11 a.m. and another church service at 12:30. We make do with what we have. We have a large city map in our office and block off bus areas. We visit every house in this area and systematically cover the city.

(7) Who works on the visitation team?

The bus captains. At times they form a whole team to visit. Each Saturday morning we have a bus meeting at 9:30 a.m. At that time we put everyone's record on the blackboard along with their weekly goals. We go over problems and answer questions. This is mainly a motivational meeting. We have found consistent visitation is the key. The captain who doesn't visit on Saturday will be down on Sunday. Many of the children come because of the bus captain.

(8) Is the competition with other busing churches difficult?

One California church goes into areas where other buses are operating and offers children bracelets if they ride their bus. We think it is wrong to take people away from another Sunday school. We are working some areas where there are four buses, some Baptist, some Church of the Nazarene, and another Church of Christ. We carefully check each home and seek those who are not attending other churches. We are a mobile society with people constantly moving in and out of neighborhoods. This is why continual contact is necessary.

Because we live in a mobile society, the concept of the community church must change. The idea that an area belongs to a certain church really goes back to when we had parishes. Many people did not have cars and we did not have freeways. They walked to the church nearest them. We do not live that way anymore. People think nothing of driving 30 miles to work or 15 miles to the super market, and, they drive to their church. With the freeways, modern communications, and with buses, people going to the church nearest them is a thing of the past.

(9) Do you stay in contact in other ways with the bus ministry?

We send out a weekly "Soul Winner" publication. This goes to everyone riding the buses. We also try to go out systematically with soul winning teams to lead parents to Christ.

(10) Do your Sunday school teachers also visit the bus children?

Yes. Even though it is a bus child and the captain is going to follow up on them, the teacher also visits. The bus captain's visitation on Saturday morning is not a real visit. The teacher must make a more meaningful contact than a casual "see you in the morning." It is a different kind of visit.

(11) How do you plan for a bus ministry?

We must be careful not to force anything. It is like forcing down the trunk on a car; something is going to be damaged. We must preach about the bus ministry, write about it, talk about it, and wait until the vision takes hold. I talked about buses for six months. I asked different people, "Would you like to drive a bus for us? Would you be a captain?" There was excitement and enthusiasm. I'll never forget the night when two fellows came into my office saying, "We've been praying with you that God would put this on someone's heart. God has put in on our hearts."

The first year we were in busing, we spent $8,000. We also increased our giving to foreign missions that year by $8,000. Thus, we did not hamper our world missionary program with our emphasis. God will be no man's debtor and we have found the people are glad to pay the bus bills when they catch the vision of winning souls through busing.

Chapter 5

HOW TO START AND MAINTAIN A BUS MINISTRY

Busing may not be for you. Most of America's large churches are engaged happily and successfully in the bus ministry; some are not. A church and a pastor should not be pressured to start busing because everybody else does it. The First Baptist Church in Dallas, Texas is one of the largest and greatest churches in the world. Yet, it is not engaged in the bus ministry. They do have a few buses, but we bring in more people on Sunday than they do.

Busing is a whole new style of operation. The Sunday morning service is different and the whole procedure of the church is changed by busing. Because busing is revolutionary, it is necessary to examine your motives. Why do you want to be involved in busing?

When the people really begin to come in and are everywhere, what are you going to do with them? What are you going to teach them? Where are you going to place them? How are you going to deal with them? It is wrong to bring them unless you can minister to them. Thus, the leadership must decide if the church is committed to evangelism, growth, and revival. Single-mindedness is the vital characteristic in building with buses. We must be sold out to winning souls.

What kind of church do you have? What is your philosophy and image? Each church develops an image. Some cater to small groups and others concern themselves with the charasmatic revival. A bus church must develop an image of being an aggressive, soul-winning church, a church committed to evangelism. Tragically, there are many who would minimize this image. A strong local church gets the job done for God. When a pastor gets so involved in trying to do the best job through the local church, he cannot go everywhere and do everything. He must stay home and build a strong church.

In developing a soul-winning image everything in the church points to evangelism, how the service is conducted, how the pastor preaches, the way he gives his altar invitation, and the way you print up your Sunday bulletin. In addition to an evangelistic Sunday morning service, you must have a strong Sunday evening emphasis and mid-week gathering. All services are geared to evangelism. From this basis it is possible to build with buses.

After philosophy, personnel is paramount. People must be recruited to build with buses who deeply believe in this ministry. Nothing matters but getting the job done. First, you need a bus captain, a bus driver, and a bus secretary. Many churches for years have had an old bus sitting out in the back and each Sunday some faithful man drives around the community to pick up a few scattered people. But, this is not a bus ministry. To move out of that dimension a bus captain is the key. He starts the bus rounds, maintains its outreach, and recruits personnel. He is the single most important person for your bus ministry. In part two of this book we describe his position and responsibilities.

The driver's responsibility is to drive and stay in the bus while the secretary takes care of records. The secretary also helps maintain order and handle discipline problems. A full breakdown of all job responsibilities will be given in part two of this book.

Where do bus workers come from? In answer, all I can say is they come from God. We refused to begin a bus ministry until we had completely shared the vision with our congregation. We talked about buses for three or four months. I talked to different people. I preached about reaching people through buses. I prayed about it. I wrote about it in our little paper. We kept the vision before the people until God gave us the personnel. It is wise to remember you can have a bus ministry without a bus quicker than you can have a bus ministry without dedicated personnel.

Because God gave us our workers, no department of our church has the record of faithfulness and loyalty that we have found in the bus ministry. God seems to reward these people in a very special way.

It is impossible to start a bus ministry unless the pastor is for it completely. The pastor who believes in a dynamic bus ministry never lets a service go by without saying something about buses. He commends a worker, notes results, or asks for help. The pastor must carry the ball if it succeeds. He is the chief motivator of the people and nothing needs as much motivation as the bus ministry. Every Saturday morning the pastor must go to the bus meeting and accompany the visitation teams. The pastor of a bus church sacrifices personal pleasure to build the kingdom. His Saturdays are key days for building with buses.

WHAT KIND OF BUSES?

"Ban the van!" Walter Beebe says. I agree. You need a big bus. We like the 66 passenger However, if it is too large for the cul de sacs and narrow streets, you might get a little smaller, a 65 passenger maybe. It makes good economic sense to get a bigger bus. You have one operation, one captain, and one insurance policy. And, it is just as easy to fill a big bus as a small one. One pastor bought a new 19 passenger bus. I feel he would have been wiser to have bought a used 66 passenger bus. We feel the larger bus is cheaper to operate in every way. We must make our dollars go as far as they can.

Appearance is important. Our buses must look good. It costs approximately $600 to replace all the windows in a bus and thus it is better to buy a bus with a good body than a bus with a good engine. Buses are getting harder and harder to find. We rented one for a while from a berry farm. But, most of the buses we have bought we have had to look diligently for. We have even had to go to the Midwest for one of our buses.

Schools have high standards so that their buses are generally in good shape when you buy them. Obviously, this is the best place to purchase if possible. But, most schools do not sell buses directly.

GETTING STARTED

Getting started in a bus ministry involves work. First, you choose an area of your town to minister. This must be an area where there are children. Map out that area and begin knocking on every door. If you canvass an area and discover another bus goes there, don't do what I almost did. When I discovered a bus was going into one housing development I almost left; gave up on that section. Then the Lord reminded me that it is our responsibility to reach the world. Whatever some other church is doing is not my responsibility. We are in one area right now with a highly productive bus route where at least three other buses go. It presents no problem. The more buses in the community, the better. People move in and out. Communities change over a period of a few weeks or months and so if you choose an area, keep working it.

After we organized we took a simple approach in our visitation. A sample conversation would be something like this. "Good morning, I'm Dan Johnson. We come by here with our Sunday school bus every Sunday and would like you to come to our church tomorrow." Response varies, but many accept our offer. Most people do not go to church. They often explain "We're Baptists" or "We're Methodists" or "We used to go, but we aren't going now." We follow up with why they ought to attend. We also give them a nice brochure of our church. Kids are the key! When we go to the communities we stop them on the street and ask them if they want to go to Sunday school. We get their names and addresses and then visit their parents. We are careful to write down their names, addresses, and phone numbers so that our bus captain will not forget them. We call the children by phone to remind them we will be by for them. This makes them feel important.

The only way to maintain a bus ministry is to visit every Saturday. In our church we have a bus meeting Saturday at 9:30 a.m. All bus workers must come and we meet for about 30 minutes. We put numbers on the blackboard showing how many each worker brought last week and give their goals for this Sunday. We outline promotions, special days coming up, and cover any questions. We pray together and by 10:00 a.m. we are on our way. On our visits we stop at every place we have riders.

On Sunday we meet at 8 a.m. to have coffee and fresh donuts. This gives drivers enough time to get the buses running right. Our bus maintenance people have already started the buses, and on Saturday had them gassed up. Our buses start rolling at 8:30. We have people placed to meet the bus people when they come in. When the children get off the buses we have a little treat for them. Every family receives the church paper and letters about special days. In the next section of this book we will spend much time outlining jobs and giving ideas. Suffice to say at this point that we believe in building with buses. Only eternity will reveal the dramatic impact busing has had on our world. I know it works from personal experience and from the testimonies of people like Bill Baker.

Today the Rev. Bill Baker is one of our most successful and progressive pastors. He has served as district youth president for the Southern Missouri District of the Assemblies of God and now leads one of the largest Indiana churches. Rev. Baker is a direct result of an effective bus ministry.

Recalling his conversion experience, Pastor Baker noted, "I was seven years old and had never been encouraged to go to Sunday school. My parents had formerly attended a Baptist Church when they lived in Arkansas. But on moving to Kansas City, Kansas, they found no Baptist Church nearby. So ours was a non-church-going home. Then one bright Sunday morning, as I was sitting on the porch of our home thinking of nothing in particular, I noticed a huge Sunday school bus pass by with these words written on it, 'Welcome to Victoria Tabernacle Sunday School.' On board were many happy young children who seemed to be very anxious to reach their destination. It aroused my curiosity to see so many young children having such a wonderful time going to church.

One day while I was playing with a boy at school he asked me whether I went to Sunday school. My answer, of course, was 'no.' Right then I made up my mind to ask my parents' permission to go to Sunday school. It took courage to ask such a question, for I was sure the answer would be negative. To my amazement, my parents consented, and the next Sunday morning I was among the many happy young children on the huge bus.

When we arrived at Sunday school, all the children knew just the right place to go. I seemed alone until the friendly bus driver put his huge hand on my shoulder and directed me to my proper department. I was very thankful for such a friendly gesture.

That first morning Sunday school made a great impression on my life. From then on I became one of the most faithful members in my Sunday school class. No more dull Sundays for me. I was always ready and waiting for that Sunday school bus.

I have earned honors for faithful attendance in Sunday school several times since. In the year 1950, a zipper Bible was awarded to me for being the only one to attend Sunday school every Sunday of that year.

I reached the age of accountability and gave my heart to the Lord. Later He called me to His service. Possibly, my life would never have been changed if it had not been for that Sunday school bus which attracted the attention of a small boy."

At Pastor Baker's church today he builds with buses. His church, Parcway Assembly, has a long and full history of reaching people for Christ. Needless to say, Pastor Baker believes in building with buses.

PART II

DEDICATED PERSONNEL

Chapter 6

THE BUS CAPTAIN

What a hen is to a brood of chickens, a lieutenant to a platoon of soldiers, a coach to a football team, a pastor to a church, so the bus captain is to the route. He is totally responsible for developing and maintaining the bus route. It is his responsibility to see that his bus is filled every Sunday and the riders safely arrive at Sunday school.

We ask our bus captains to see that pupils find their classes and new visitors are properly introduced. The captain also assumes the responsibility of seeing the children get back on the bus after church and arrive home safely. The captain is totally responsible for everything that happens on his route. Because it is such a heavy responsibility we ask the captains to work under the pastor or the full-time church bus director. We help him supervise the driver, bus secretary, and workers.

WHO IS A BUS CAPTAIN?

The success of a bus ministry depends on the

faithfulness of bus captains. Therefore, he must be chosen carefully and trained. Perhaps it would be well to ask "Who is a bus captain?" In trying to answer that question I think of the persons involved in our own bus ministry. Stan Martin, our first captain, was not even living for the Lord when he first came to our church. One evening after service he called me down the hall and asked if I would pray with him. He said, "I haven't really been living like I should. I want to dedicate my life to Christ." That night became a turning point in Stan's life.

Stan Martin faithfully worked with us. He prayed and participated in all our soul-winning endeavors. God began to put a special burden on Stan's heart. After we had prayed, talked about, and written about busing, Stan responded. He became our first bus captain. He is a young man with a wife and family. He is a typical bus captain.

The bus work is not confined to me. Paula is another excellent bus captain. She was reached as a direct result of one of our buses. One of our members stopped at her house and won her to the Lord. Paula came to our church and was filled with the Holy Spirit. She wanted to be a strong witness for the Master and felt the bus ministry the best way to do this. She has done an outstanding job, although she is a very busy woman in her everyday life.

Two years ago, Steve Rogers was a long-haired rebel. He came to our church at the invitation of a couple of friends. He was gloriously saved and his life totally changed. We needed a new bus captain and Steve, along with his young wife,

Judy, accepted the challenge. They have been very faithful and today form one of our strongest evangelistic teams.

At Spanaway the bus captain is chosen with care from among faithful, devoted, and concerned church members. They are people who really love God. Sex and age are not really important in choosing bus captains. We believe age is less important than character in selecting a captain who is responsible for bringing 40 to 50 people to Sunday school each Sunday. We have captains who are teenagers, some who are young married couples and work as teams, while others are single adults. We have a number of middle-aged couples involved as captains. Some churches feel teenagers are too young to handle such responsibility. We do not. We choose by Christian character and compassion before sex and age. It is urgent that a captain be faithful to the work of God. Paul says clearly, "Moreover it is required in stewards, that a man be found faithful." (I Corinthians 4:2)

Somebody asked me "If you were starting out in the bus ministry all over again, what is the first thing you would do?" After careful consideration I feel the most important thing is to discover whether the church has an all-out commitment to evangelism. It is absolutely essential that everyone in the church be committed to winning the lost. Next, and almost of equal importance is finding people who will assume the responsibility and carry the load. As we have said before, you can have a bus ministry without a bus much quicker than you can have a bus ministry with a bus, but without proper personnel.

TRAINING THE CAPTAIN

Regardless of how good a person is, he must be trained. We carefully tell the new recruit that the most important person involved in this ministry is the captain. We share information about his responsibility in seeing things are done right. We have already screened him so we know the validity of his conversion experience. We are careful that he understands our basic doctrine since he is the one representing our church. We insist he be a member of the church and one who believes in what our church stands for. We require him to be faithful to the church, loyal to his pastor and leadership of the Sunday school. The bus captain must attend all church services unless prevented by work responsibilities.

In orientating our captains we go through our whole procedures with them. We show him the large map on one wall in our office which outlines our bus routes. We tell him his assignment and block off the entire area. He is asked to recruit helpers and to knock on every door in that area. He takes your literature from the church with him telling the parents what their children will be learning in the Sunday school. The captain is told to give each parent a card saying when the child is picked up and brought home. We pray with each new recruit and then stay with him as he begins his new adventure in witnessing.

PROPER TRAINING

Telling what to do is not enough. We have found we must show the new captain how to become an effective worker. Therefore, the pastor or an experienced bus worker goes with him to show him how it is done. He learns by doing more than by our telling him. A typical conversation the recruit and the veteran bus worker might encounter would be:

"Good morning. I am Stan Martin from Spanaway Assembly. We come by here every Sunday morning with our Sunday school bus and pick up children and families and take them to our Sunday school and back. Do you attend Sunday school regularly?"

If the answer is "yes" the new bus captain recruit is taught to respond "That's wonderful. We're not trying to take people away from any other church. Thank you for your time."

There are thousands of people in all communities who do not go to any church. If the people visited are not involved in a Bible-believing church we might be able to reach them later after getting other riders in the neighborhood. The main thing is to assure the prospects that the church is seeking to reach those not already committed. The bus captain is taught to congratulate the people for going to church, invite them to visit sometime, and let it go at that.

Most people visited do not attend church. If the people do not attend church anywhere we ask the new captain to say "We'd love to come by and pick you up. Our bus comes right by the door, and I will come right to your door and pick you up and the children up. We'll come by about 9:15. Is that okay?" If it appears the children will be the ones riding the new captain is taught to talk to them. We have found it important to converse directly with the children to let them know we are interested in them personally.

Several things should be in these visits. The first is that the church is interested in people. Then, it is necessary to emphasize your church teaches the Bible and morality. We have discovered when people are not familiar with our church, or even oppose our denomination it is good to emphasize our teaching of the Bible. This is our real selling point. Our captains are taught to emphasize, "Look, we teach the Bible and we teach morality. This is what our children need, isn't it?" These statements bring few arguments. It is also important to say the buses are driven by properly licensed and competent adults. Captains are also told to stress the safety factors. Each bus is properly licensed, maintained, and insured. The children are under adult supervision at all times. Emphasis should be made that the captains pick the children up and bring them back. We tell our workers to make much of the fact that they care for the children and they are responsible.

When the prospects decide to attend the captains are instructed to bring out the records. Our church uses a triplicate form which makes the whole job of record-keeping easy. (Samples of our bus forms are pictured in this manual.) Family information is gleaned with careful notes of all children's names. It is difficult on Sunday morning to find out the child's name. Sometimes he is not even old enough to know his full name. So, at this time, when the captain talks to the parent, he gets the names, birthdays, address, and phone number.

THE CAPTAIN ON SUNDAY MORNING

Bus captains must not only fill buses; they must see that riders are safe and happy. Activities should be planned on the bus trips. If the distance between the homes and church is great the captains might want to have singing and a little service on the bus. Games can be planned and other activities to keep riders busy. If the bus route is in the general neighborhood of the church there is not enough time for much activity. It is important simply to keep everybody happy and safe. Children must not be allowed to stand while the vehicle is in motion. Of course, there can be no fighting. We have found it necessary to see that older children do not pick on the little kids. This is very frightening to little ones seated on a large and strange bus. Proper discipline must be assured if the route grows. Nothing can kill a route quicker than a rowdy route.

Our captains know and keep a rigid time schedule. When they arrive with their load at the church they have someone help them get the little children to their Sunday school classes. We control traffic in several ways. Sometimes we stamp the number of the child's bus on his hand. Other times we pin information on his lapel. Some captains like to identify their children with flags or small lapel pins. Careful planning here can prevent children missing their buses home creating tension for all involved. The bus captain can make the teacher's work light. It is important the captains and the Sunday school teachers work together. The captain is careful to emphasize that everybody riding his bus must go to Sunday school and church. They are required to stay for all of the services. Teenagers especially will ride the bus and then want to go to a nearby store or elsewhere. We do not permit this and the bus captain is a key to stopping these problems.

Following the Sunday services the bus captain goes to the classrooms to help the youngsters return to the buses. It is important that the children file from their classrooms to the buses in an orderly fashion. Just before our buses leave, our bus captains pick up a sack of candy for their bus children. As the children get off the bus each child is given a piece of candy. This leaves a sweet taste in their mouths in more than one way and we think it is important.

Our bus captains return to each home with the children. This responsibility is never left to the bus driver. The captain is careful the children do not dart in front of the bus or go alone to their front doors. We teach our captains that their responsibility is from the front door back to the front door. This shows parents that their children's safety is important to us.

WEEKLY MEETINGS

Every Saturday we have a bus meeting at 9:30 a.m. This is designed with 30 minutes of inspiration and motivation. We answer questions, make announcements for our promotions, and provide literature to be passed out. Then we go over what each bus captain did the previous Sunday. We post his goals for the next day, Sunday. All do better when they have a definable and visible goal. In sharing these goals with others they are under pressure to actualize them. These meetings, we have found, keep workers from becoming slothful and negligent.

After our half hour of inspiration, motivation, and instruction we have a short prayer together. Then we go out on visitation. We have found it takes approximately three hours to cover a route of normal length. Our contacts are simple brief reminders to our riders that we will pick them up the following morning. We take this time to also inquire about bus absentees the previous Sunday.

A church cannot pick up large numbers of people from all kinds of homes each week without having some problems. Occasionally, we lose a child. When that happens we usually find the child has gotten on the wrong bus. Sometimes fighting or some other problem arises. It is important in your weekly visitation to discover and report any problems to the pastor or director of the bus ministry. The captain should remember that his responsibility is a heavy one and he assumes a full load. He is responsible to God, to the pastor, to the Sunday school, and to the church for those persons under his care.

We try to encourage our captains to understand their spiritual responsibility. They must love the children, pray for them, and remember the ultimate objective of a bus ministry is to get the entire family saved.

Chapter 7

THE BUS DRIVER

There could be no bus route in any church if it were not for the faithful services of the men and women who drive the buses. We must never overlook the tremendous contribution these make to an effective bus ministry.

Before discussing the responsibilities of drivers, it might be well to remind ourselves of Paul's discussion of the body of Christ. He said, "Now there are diversities of gifts, but the same Spirit. And there are differences of administrations, but it is the same God which worketh all in all." (I Corinthians 12:4-6)

In this dynamic scripture Paul goes on to add, "For as the body is one, and hath many members, and all the members of that one body, being many, are one body: so also is Christ. For by one Spirit are we all baptized into one body, whether we be Jews or Gentiles, whether we be bond or free; and have been all made to drink into one Spirit. For the body is not one member, but many." (I Corinthians 12:15)

Paul talks frankly about jealousy in the ministry

and dissatisfaction with one's task by adding, "If the foot shall say, Because I am not the hand, I am not of the body; is it therefore not of the body? And if the ear shall say, Because I am not the eye, I am not of the body; is it therefore not of the body? If the whole body were an eye, where were the hearing? If the whole were hearing, where were the smelling? But now hath God set the members every one of them in the body, as it hath pleased him. And if they were all one member, where were the body? But now are they many members, yet but one body. And the eye cannot say unto the hand, I have no need of thee: nor again the head to the feet, I have no need of you. Nay, much more those members of the body, which seem to be more feeble, are necessary:" (I Corinthians 12:15-22) I feel a good understanding of the importance of every job is necessary for us who are involved in the bus ministry. While the bus captain has the most important job in the bus ministry, the driver also plays an important part in this work.

WHO ARE THE DRIVERS?

We believe bus drivers should be believers. Some churches do not follow this stipulation, but we have found it important. He must love the Lord for this is no routine job. Bus driving is a ministry. In our church the driver not only drives, but also participates in our Saturday visitation.

There is another reason we feel our drivers must know the Lord. Many of our bus children come from broken homes. Others have never had a proper male image. In their homes they may never have seen a man who is kind, tender-hearted, or caring. We want these children to identify with our bus drivers. We want our drivers to be faithful every Sunday. We feel it is not good for many different people to drive a bus. The children need familiar and friendly faces as they get on the buses. They recognize the driver and receive a smile and warm greetings. This is most meaningful to our riders. So, the bus driver is a committed Christian who loves the Lord, loves children, and is a soul-winner.

Bus drivers must be vitally interested in the work of God. A great deal of time is required in this job with many sacrifices. Some of our drivers do not eat Sunday dinner until 3:00 p.m. This is a sacrifice for them and their families, yet they never complain. There is great satisfaction involved in doing the work of God.

RESPONSIBILITIES OF DRIVERS

What are the responsibilities of the driver? First, the bus is in his responsibility. The driver makes sure the bus is ready to go each Sunday morning. The director of maintenance sees that the bus is swept out during the week and running. But, regardless of whose responsibilities some of these things happen to be, the driver must know these things are done. The driver arrives early on Sunday morning to get the bus warmed. On the previous days he has made sure the bus is gassed up, the oil is checked, and is ready to be operated in a safe manner.

The driver works very close with the bus captain. The driver recognizes the captain is responsible for the whole operation and so he follows instructions of his leader. We have had little trouble in this chain of authority. Together the driver and captain can develop a fine team spirit.

Each state has its own laws concerning the operation of buses. Drivers should have a state manual so they understand all the laws governing bus operation. This can be obtained from the state capitol or license burėau. Some states require a special chaffeur's license for drivers while others do not. Special insurance is required by other states. Beyond the specific rules and regulations differing in each state, there are certain principles common to all.

COMMON SAFETY FEATURES

The bus driver must be taught to come to a complete stop at all railroad crossings. He must use his signals properly and when he backs up the bus he must be careful. We ask the bus captain to step to the back of the bus and help the driver in backing up. This is risky and bus accidents occur here. We are careful that our bus drivers become "professional" in the handling of these machines. After all, we are handling the most precious cargo of all: human lives.

A driver should never leave his bus while it is running. This is why it is necessary to have both a captain and a driver for every vehicle. We never let a bus driver go alone. There are just too many risks involved in doing so. The driver is asked to be sure the back door of his bus is secured. All windows must be up during the run.

Children stay seated and the captain maintains order on the bus. The driver is not to talk with children once the bus starts rolling. He stays with the bus at the church and doesn't leave it until everyone is gone. Any problems here are passed on to the bus captain.

It would be impossible to say too much about safety. When the bus pulls away from the church there are 40 to 70 lives in our care. We must be aware of our tremendous responsibility. The driver is careful to maintain proper speed, obey all traffic signals, and take every precaution so that no one is injured as a result of some error.

After his run on Sunday, the driver sees that the bus is properly parked, windows are shut, lights extinguished, ignition turned off, and the bus is locked up. Any malfunctions of the bus are noted by the driver for the maintenance people.

The bus driver's job may not seem glamorous, but it is urgently important. At Spanaway we give great honor to these men and women who keep our buses rolling in very practical ways.

Chapter 8

THE BUS WORKER

Much teamwork is required to develop and maintain the bus ministry. Often churches have little success with their bus ministries because they do not have enough personnel in the program. In addition to our captains and drivers, we have workers, secretaries, and maintenance people. The bus worker is a very important member of our team.

The bus worker can act as assistant to the captain, mechanic, one who cleans the bus, a cook who prepares breakfast on special days for other bus workers, or a substitute driver. In our ministry many of our captains have developed teams of workers who go with them in their weekly visitation and help recruit new drivers.

Working directly under the bus captain, the worker must be a highly dependable person. We require that they be drawn from among the faithful and born-again men and women of our congregation.

Bus workers must be inspired to do their work by the pastor. If the pastor is not committed to a bus outreach, workers are difficult to recruit. However, when the pastor underscores the importance of bus work, praising the workers in it, helps raise funds for new buses, and reinforces this program, workers volunteer. So the pastor is really the key person in recruiting and sustaining bus workers.

RECRUITING WORKERS

Most of our bus workers come as the result of a pastoral message on evangelism. Many have come straight out of the prayer room to respond to an appeal for workers. Also, we actively recruit helpers by personal contact. Some churches place cards in each hymnal rack on which interested persons write their names if they want to volunteer for a ministry. We also have sent personal letters to persons inviting them to get involved in our work. Then, we pray for workers. It should be noted that the only prayer request Jesus ever made was when He said "pray ye therefore the Lord of the harvest, that he will send forth labourers into his harvest." (Matthew 9:38)

Workers we enlist may be faithful as long as they are in sympathy with us, we motivate them, or as long as we are involved in the work. However, workers the Holy Spirit inspires will work against all odds and in every situation. In our church we have noticed a great degree of faithfulness and loyalty to the work of God among our bus workers. I deeply believe this is because these people have come directly from the prayers we prayed for workers.

Some of our best workers have been new Christians. We find they do not know any better than to get involved in the work of reaching other people for Christ. They are so happy to be saved from a life of darkness that they are proud to be a part of a soul-winning program, sharing Christ with others, for Jesus Christ.

JOB DESCRIPTIONS

As with all bus personnel, we have found proper training of workers vital. Therefore, we prepare a job description for every member of our team. The job descriptions we use are included in the last part of this book. We carefully explain the responsibility of each person and to whom they are responsible. We also suggest how they should dress, how to keep proper records and so on. It is important to make our workers feel secure in their ministry. We place a heavy emphasis on training for we have seen too many bus ministries die because workers are recruited for a job and left without instructions. They get frustrated, discouraged, and even resentful without proper help.

Care must also be taken to give workers the scriptural imperative of their job. We remind them how often Jesus Christ commanded us to go with the Gospel. We say Christ never suggested that sinners come to the church, but that we should go to where sinners are. We take our workers to bus clinics and workshops to help them understand their great spiritual task. We often invite someone to our church who has a successful bus program. They inspire our people. We also provide good literature on the subject of busing so our helpers can be constantly encouraged and inspired to do their best for God.

A HIGHLY SUCCESSFUL PLAN

We have been highly successful with bus workers. Our captains often select teenagers and train them to become bus captains. One of the most important results of this is that when we need new bus captains, we find them already trained among our workers. Most of our present captains were once bus workers serving under someone else.

It is one of our greatest joys to see how God uses these bus workers in wonderful ways. They are always so willing to do the small but necessary tasks of this great ministry. They are helpers in the truest sense and are as important in the body of Christ as a pastor. There people are key in the work of God.

When we get to Heaven I am sure great rewards will be given to many people from churches who have not taken any prominent or public place. Maybe they are not known by many. Yet, they have been faithful, dependable, and available to do what they could do to keep the work of God moving so successfully. Thank God for good bus workers.

Chapter 9

THE BUS SECRETARY

Many executives say a good secretary is worth far more to their business than highly paid assistants. This is certainly true in the bus ministry. It is necessary that each bus route have its own secretary. In addition, then, to the captain, the driver, and the workers, we have a bus secretary.

Our bus secretaries are chosen as all other workers in this ministry. They are born again and faithful in their lives. We look for loyal members of our church and those who love lost souls to serve as secretaries. Secretaries may be teenagers, or the wives of other bus workers. The main thing is they know how to keep accurate records.

We want our bus secretaries to know our bus children on a personal basis, rather than just as a name on a form. Therefore, we encourage them to get involved on the bus route in a very practical way. They are required to ride the buses and very often the secretary will assist the captain in the weekly visitation or other activities.

DUTIES OUTLINED

We have outlined various duties for our bus secretaries. They are:

1. He or she will keep accurate records of all the children who attend.
2. The secretary helps keep order on the bus.
3. The secretary files her weekly report of statistics to the pastor or bus director. On this record what time the bus left the church, how many visits were made, what time they returned, how many passengers came, how many first time visitors, and any difficulties for their bus work are listed.

Many churches use a triplicate form. There is a sample of this form pictured in this book. It can be ordered from Gospel Publishing House, 1445 Boonville Ave., Springfield, Mo. 65802. Many other publishers have similar forms for this use.

We insist each secretary secures as much information about each child as possible. Since the best time to get this information is during the Saturday morning visits. We want our secretaries along on these visitations if possible. Many times it is necessary to talk to the mother or father to get the correct spelling of names, address, and the correct telephone number and birthdate. We have found parents more free to share this information with a bus secretary than a male bus captain.

Our secretaries fill out triplicate forms for each child. When the child boards the bus information is secured from him if it has not already been secured the day before. Children are carefully counted for and records are made. One copy of this form goes with the student to his Sunday school class. This helps identify each child and know the new ones. A second copy goes to the central office of the Sunday school where total records are kept for all those who attend. The third copy is kept by the captain. This helps the captain keep accurate records of visits, persons who ride, the number of Sundays they ride his bus, and absentees.

We ask our bus secretary to take a head count on the buses each week. This may seem to duplicate the bus captain's work, but we find it very helpful. She takes the count before they leave the bus at Sunday school and again before they leave the church. We like the security of this double check.

A WORD ABOUT RECORDS

High on the list of reasons for failure of a busing business is inadequate records. It is impossible to be totally honest without keeping complete and accurate records. We know God keeps a record. The Bible tells us the time will come when every one will give an account to Him of our thoughts, words, and motives.

Without keeping careful records it is difficult to know where we have been, where we are going, and even where we are now. In record keeping, there are a number of things in which we are vitally interested. First, we want the record of attendance or absence of every regular bus rider. We also want the total number of riders on a given Sunday. To see how faithful we are we keep a number of our visitations, the hours we spend in visiting, and number of new riders who come. We feel it important to know how much the bus ministry costs, so we keep accurate record of fuel and maintenance costs.

The bus secretary is a vital part of our success. We do not have all these positions just for "busy work" or to give people jobs. We feel each position vital and we could not operate our program without them.

Chapter 10

PROMOTIONS AND CONTESTS

Bus pastors believe in contests. We are all aware of the classic arguments between the merits of intrinsic and extrinsic motivation. Men with greater minds than ours have debated the question throughout the centuries. Suffice for us to say that to operate a successful busing program one must have promotion and contest.

Intrinsic motivation is certainly a factor after conversion, but we must remember we are basically dealing with the unconverted. We have to get them in to our church so we can introduce them to Christ. When Christ enters them they then can be intrinsically motivated. Therefore, we have contests without apology, for we believe in promotion.

Jesus himself says that he who gives a cup of cold water to someone in Christ's name will not lose his reward. And, we do not object to any legitimate means, within good taste, to induce people to come to the house of God.

We feel we have good Biblical basis for the contests among our workers also. Christians all look forward to the day when we shall stand before the judgment seat of Christ and receive our rewards. We preach about these things. Surely, there is nothing wrong in this. The Bible says every man shall receive praise from God.

We believe in promotion. However, we must underscore that a bus ministry cannot be perpetuated on contests, gimmicks, and give-aways. If it is then one finds his church competing against other churches giving bigger prizes. Our ministry is maintained through faithful prayer, sacrificial efforts, and faithful visitation. There is no other way to keep it going.

Probably no other ministry needs more promotion and motivation than the bus outreach. The bus ministry is very difficult. The riders of our buses are children from non-Christian homes. In many cases the children would not come unless they wanted to themselves. It is up to us to see that children want to come to our church. We have to make Sunday school fun and exciting.

At Spanaway we have two kinds of contests. One is for the bus personnel, while the other is for the children. Children's contests run almost continually. But, only about twice a year do we stage a contest for workers.

Recently we had a contest for bus captains. The prize was a weekend trip for two from Seattle to Spokane to attend one of the progressive churches there. Mike and Kathy Merrich won the contest. They flew to Spokane for the weekend and had an exciting time. They also were able to observe another great church in action.

Among other contests we have is one in which we award a captain a red blazer when he has brought one hundred on his bus. Three of our captains have earned this blazer and wear it proudly. We make this presentation a big affair before the entire congregation.

One time our bus director made a foolish promise. He promised the bus captains that if any had over 100 on a bus on a given Sunday he would swallow a goldfish. To his dismay, one of the captains reached the 100 mark and he had to swallow the fish. He has not made such a promise since.

Each bus captain can have a contest with the children on his own bus. Or, it is possible to have a contest for all of the children on all the buses. Last summer we said all who rode on a given Sunday would be taken the following Friday to see the Tacoma Twins play baseball. We had a record attendance that Sunday. When Friday night came we had six large buses running down the freeway carrying several hundred children and their parents. This was very effective.

We often have a "Watermelon Sunday." All who come on this day in August are given a piece of watermelon. It is one of the most effective things we have done. It is really simple and inexpensive. Our helpers cut the watermelon and every child was given a nice slice of juicy, chilled melon when he left the bus.

There are many other promotional ideas. Many promotional books are on the market to assist in selecting the right promotion for each church. Creativity counts. The children are out there to be reached for Christ. Let us rise to the challenge and bring in as many as possible for Christ.

Recently the National Sunday School Department of the Assemblies of God listed some policies and ideas for promotions and contests. Here is what they suggest:

> Kids love contests and treats. All of these, properly used, are helpful in building attendance, attracting new riders, and communicating to the children that you really like them. However, two cautionary statements are in order:
>
> 1. Don't attempt continuous contests or big promotions every Sunday. A small treat each week, such as a piece of candy, as the child leaves the bus is fine. However, if you promote big every Sunday you will not have anything exciting when you plan a big day.
>
> 2. Don't allow yourself to become competetive with other evangelical churches. Attempts to outdo other bus ministries with bigger treats and bigger prizes will soon bring diminishing returns. It does not instill loyalty in the children. They will begin to wait and see who is giving the best prize or treat before they decide which bus to ride.

Generally it is better to give several small prizes that many people can win instead of one "super" prize to the person who brings the most.

Don't overlook prizes and recognition gifts to your bus workers. Award them a "fishers of men" pin or blazer with appropriate insignia when they reach 75 or 100 riders on their route. Appropriate prizes for contests between your bus captains are free trips to national or regional bus conventions or clinics.

Promotions involve many different incentives to people to be in attendance and to bring others with them for a particular day. This may include contests and give-aways but usually involves some special attraction as well. Here are some successful promotions which have been used.

Special guests:

Cowboy and his horse
A clown
The great pumpkin
Snoopy, Charlie Brown and other characters
Christian athlete
Midget
Giant

McDonald Sunday, complete with Ronald McDonald, and a stop at McDonald's on the way home for a hamburger and soft drink is one of the most consistently popular promotions.

Sustained promotions which require loyalty over a period of weeks are good. These include:

Ten commandment key chain or charm bracelet
Twelve apostles key chain or charm bracelet
My Picture Book

Each of these sustained promotions require the pupil to be present over a period of several weeks in order to acquire a complete set of ten commandment or apostle charms. My Picture Book is a simple photo album with places for pictures of the church, Jesus, the pastor, bus captain, Sunday school teacher, etc. Each Sunday one of the pictures is given to be placed in the album.

Breakfast on the bus (milk and donuts) is not only a promotional "gimmick" but in many poorer neighborhoods an actual ministry. Many of these children are hungry, especially on Sunday morning when Mom and Dad "sleep in." Bus captains have commented on the improved behavior when the children received a light snack. Hungry children are not ready learners.

Special days include the obvious Christmas, Easter, Mother's Day, etc., but how about trying:

Election day—Use simulated ballots as promotional handouts. Don't vote for the devil by staying home—vote for Jesus—be in Sunday school.

Pastor's Birthday—Complete with a huge cake and candles to be shared by all the children (the cake, not the candles).

Picture Day—Have a photographer on hand to take group pictures of the buses, workers, and riders. Also each of the Sunday school classes. It will get them there one Sunday to have their picture taken and another Sunday in order to receive a copy of the picture.

Bounce back Sunday—Perfect ending to a summer slump. And what better give-away than a rebound top (yo-yo) with your church name printed on it?

Giant Sunday—Feature everything big. World's biggest popcorn ball, longest candy bar, biggest snowcone, etc.

Give-aways are special prizes or treats given to everyone in attendance on a given Sunday. Here is a list of popular items.

1. Goldfish
2. Snowcones
3. Flags
4. Kites
5. Yo-yos
6. Pictures
7. Cupcakes
8. Popsicles
9. Candy bars
10. Pens
11. Pencils
12. Key chains
13. Pony rides
14. Ice cream bars
15. Flowers
16. Bibles
17. Bats
18. Balls
19. Badges
20. Hot dogs
21. Soft drinks
22. Indian headdresses
23. Decals
24. Watermelon
25. Popcorn balls
26. Picnic

Keep in mind that simple prizes promoted with enthusiasm by the pastor, Sunday school teacher, and bus captain will produce better results than many larger prizes.

PART III

FORMS AND POLICY INSTRUCTIONS USED BY SPANAWAY ASSEMBLY

POLICY INSTRUCTION

Subject:

The Bus Captain

Your Route in General

1. The success or failure of a bus route depends upon the commitment of the Bus Captain. This is basically a spiritual commitment.

2. The Bus Captain is completely responsible for the bus ministry in his or her assigned area.

3. The Bus Captain is to see that his bus is filled with people every week. It requires a definite minimum of three (3) hours of visitation each week.

4. It should be understood that many of the riders will be children.

5. The position of Bus Captain falls under the general responsibility of the Bus Director.

6. The Bus Captain is required to attend all the public services of our church, including Sunday school, morning and evening services and the midweek services. Attendance at special services or revivals is also required. "Moreover it is required in stewards (bus captains) that a man be found faithful" I Corinthians 4:2.

7. The selection of the personnel to assist the Bus Captain in their visitation and work must be first approved by the Bus Director. If the Bus Captain has a prospective worker in mind he should have the prospect "cleared" by the Bus Director BEFORE asking them to help in the program.

8. All bus workers are asked to attend the Teachers' and Officers' Meeting each Wednesday at 7:00 p.m., meeting in the East Wing.

9. Bus Captains are responsible to see that their team is informed of the procedures and rules of the bus program of our church. Should a problem develop the Captain should attempt to deal with it while it is small and can be handled easily and quickly.

Your Visitation Responsibilities:

1. All Bus Captains are required to attend the Bus Workers meeting at 9:30 a.m. each Saturday. Because of the importance of this meeting a special attempt should be made to be in attendance each week.

2. You are to visit the houses and people in the area assigned to you.

A. In establishing or maintaining a route it is necessary to go door-to-door combing the area for people who do not attend church.

B. Leave a "We Love Children" brochure at each new house.

C. After the route is established and a person rides your bus, each and every Saturday you are to revisit and recommit that person for the following Sunday. This is a must.

D. The object of the visit is to commit people to ride your bus on Sunday. Of course, if the opportunity presents itself, try to meet any need you may discover. Remember, your Saturday visitation is to commit riders for the next day.

E. From our experiences, Saturday has been found to be the best day for visitation. If you visit earlier in the week, you are to be sure that all of your riders are contacted by phone on Saturday night to remind the rider.

3. Use your assistant captain, workers, secretary, etc. to assist you in visitation. This not only multiplies your efforts, but also provides an opportunity for them to learn how to build and maintain a route.

4. The approach at the door could be personally developed by you or you could use the one suggested elsewhere in this manual. However, there are a few very important facts which should be shared at each door if at all possible. Some are:

A. Introduce self.

B. Be gracious; speak clearly and audibly.

C. The buses are driven by competent, properly licensed and insured drivers—as required by laws.

D. The buses are fully insured and maintained so that they are safe and clean for the riders.

E. Explain that all the children are under adult supervision from the time they leave home until they return.

F. Tell as much about our Sunday school and church program as is possible.

G. Fill out a triplicate form for each rider and the time of commitment.

5. Do not let unkind and critical remarks discourage you. Expect an objection at each door. (They usually have one or they would already be in church.) Be prepared, but not defensive.

6. It is good to keep a record of all visits made; even those who do not respond to our invitations.

7. You must contact the Bus Director at least 24 hours in advance of absence (Thursday evenings) so that he can find or approve a replacement for you. In case of sickness or emergency the Bus Director should be contacted as soon as possible.

8. Captains are required to wear "church type" clothing at all times when working on a route. Dress slacks and sport shirts should be worn by the men. Ties are encouraged for Sunday mornings. Slacks or shorts are never acceptable apparel for the ladies. The ladies must never wear low cut clothing or short skirts.

Your Records:

1. Each Captain should have a secretary to assist him on his route. The policies for secretaries are found elsewhere in this manual.

2. Complete a triplicate form in its entirety for each rider at the time of enlistment of the rider.

3. When the riders get on board the bus on Sunday, give them the yellow copy. They are then to give it to their Sunday school class teacher.

4. The blue copy is forwarded to the Bus Director.

5. The card-stock copy is retained by you so that you may take attendance each week.

6. Your route book should be maintained so that the records are in the order in which you plan to pick up the riders on Sunday. This will enable another person, in an emergency, to run your route, using your route book, without much difficulty.

7. You are to record the facts of your bus route each Sunday on the Bus Ministry Weekly Report form which is in the Sunday school office. This is to be completed before going to Sunday school class each week.

8. Although some of these responsibilities can be handled by a secretary, it is understood that the Bus Captain should see that they are carried out each week.

Sunday Morning Responsibilities

1. You will need to leave the church in time to make your run and return to the church by 9:40 for Sunday School "A" and by 11:10 for Sunday School "B". Coffee and donuts are available in the East Wing from 8:00 - 8:30 a.m.

2. You are to be sure your drivers and helpers are on time.

3. You need at least one adult or older high-school teen with you. This will help you greatly. The only requirements for these helpers are: They must be saved and living a consistent Christian life; "cleared" by Bus Director; informed of Bus Ministry Rules and Procedures; cooperative and faithful.

4. Go to the door to help each rider get on the bus.

5. You are responsible to get children across street safely to the bus and back to their house. Never let them go alone; either at pick-up or delivery.

6. Never let a child get off at the corner. Never have a child meet you at a corner. Always go to the house—pick-up and delivery.

7. Take attendance record of each rider on bus each week.

8. Maintain discipline on you bus at all times. Every child must be seated at all times, if possible. Should some need to stand (as is often the case) select the older children and instruct them to hold on to a seat or bar. There should be no screaming or shouting at any time. Sometimes singing will pleasantly eliminate this problem. Absolutely no fighting. Look for those who "pick on" other riders and isolate them.

9. Be sure all children get to their proper classrooms. All new riders MUST have the yellow form with them.

10. Some parents will pick their children up after Sunday school. This is not recommended, but if this does occur insist on being informed about it. A student may not go home with anyone other than a parent with whom they live unless a WRITTEN notice from parent is presented to the captain. Word-of-mouth from parent is NOT sufficient. This is very important.

11. All Bus Captains are required to attend Sunday school class, teach a class, etc. or other places of responsibility. The Bus Director should be informed of any jobs (teaching, assisting, monitoring, etc.) taken by Bus Captains.

12. The rules of the Bus Program should be explained to the riders at least every other week:

A. They must attend class and church.
B. No gum chewing
C. No fighting
D. No talking when a teacher or worker is talking.
E. Rules must be obeyed on buses, etc.

13. Tell the children each week before they leave the bus to go to their classes which bus they should load back on. Either a number (for "A") or a flag color (for "B").

14. Everyone, including the Bus Captain, must be seated if at all possible when the bus is moving. No one should talk with the driver except that which is necessary for the operation of the bus.

<u>When the Church Service is Over</u>:

1. Go to each classroom for smaller children and assist them in finding the bus or arrange for this to be done by the secretary or helper.

2. Count heads before leaving. Go over roster if you are short a rider or two. Should a child be apparently lost, do not spend an exaggerated amount of time looking for them. Take the other riders home first. Explain to the parent of the lost child that they probably got on a wrong bus and that you will personally bring home their child by car. When the child is found phone the parent immediately.

3. Go to the bus as soon as possible. Do not linger and talk with others.

4. Candy will be bagged for you each week and ready for you in the Sunday school office. The candy should be given to each rider as they get off the bus.

5. The Captain is required to be on the bus to return the children each week. There will be no exceptions to this rule.

Suggestions:

1. Treasure your bus record book. Guard it with your life.

2. Turn in written reports as suggested by the Bus Director.

3. Report any problems of any nature to the Bus Director.

4. Know the responsibilities of each of the workers, secretaries, etc. and help them with their jobs.

5. Read this manual periodically.

6. Pray before you begin. Pray while you visit. Pray when you pick them up. Pray while you are in church. Pray while you return. Pray all week long. Pray, pray, pray.

POLICY INSTRUCTION

Subject:

The Bus Driver

Assume the attitude, "This is my bus that my church gave me to use in serving my Lord."

1. Make sure the bus is clean inside before beginning a route. If not, please sweep it out.

2. Check to see that the gas tank is filled before each trip.

3. Check oil and water each week.

4. Arrive early on Sunday (15 - 30 minutes) and start your bus. (They have been known to not start.)

5. The Bus Driver should know that the captain is responsible for the entire operation of the route, and that he is to follow the captain's directions. Help develop a "team spirit."

6. The driver must at all times observe speed limits and other traffic regulations.

7. The driver must stop at each Railroad Crossing whether riders are on board or not. The door should be opened to listen for a train and then proceed with caution. Do not shift when crossing

the tracks. Use a gear so shifting will not be necessary. This rule must be obeyed at ALL railroads marked by signals or not.

8. The driver is never to leave the bus when riders are on board, unless in an emergency. Never leave the bus when motor is running.

9. In case of emergency, pull off right-of-way as far as possible, park bus, set brake, turn off engine. Do not allow anyone off the bus unless they are in danger because of the location of the bus. Summons help by phoning the church as quickly as possible.

10. When turning a corner or passing over a rough road, the children's comfort and safety should always be considered.

11. Always allow adequate time to gear the bus down to a complete stop when approaching an intersection or traffic signal.

12. Never back the bus—unless someone is directing you from outside the bus.

13. At the end of each Sunday, the drivers of each bus should make sure the buses are properly parked and secured. (All electricity off, windows closed, emergency brake set, doors closed, etc.)

14. Never give assistance to a motorist, even from our own church. You have too much responsibil-

ity of your own.

15. Discourage anyone who is not properly licensed and "cleared" by the Bus Director from starting, warming up or driving the bus even in our church parking areas.

16. Start turn signals 100 feet before turn. Make sure signals are turned off after turn is made.

17. Keep order on the bus at all times. Never allow the passengers to distract your attention.

18. Before each trip, make sure the back door of your bus will open.

19. Allow passengers to cross in front of bus. Make sure the captain or worker assists the child across the street.

20. Make sure the bus is ready to go on time each Sunday.

21. Be courteous to the parents and the children.

22. Be at your bus while it is loading after church.

23. Turn in written reports as requested by the Bus Director.

24. Attend meetings for the bus workers when requested by the Bus Director.

25. Report any problems to the Bus Director.

26. Contact the Bus Director at least 24 hours in advance of absence.

27. The Bus Drivers are required to attend all the public services of our church, including Sunday school, morning and evening services and the mid-week services. Attendance at special services or revivals is also required. "Moreover it is required in stewards (bus drivers) that a man be found faithful" I Corinthians 4:2.

28. Drivers are to fill out the "Bus Work Sheet" on any and all maintenance which needs to be done. (No verbal orders) This form is to be given to the Director of Bus Maintenance.

29. If a driver picks up the children on a Sunday morning, they are expected to drive that same route home.

30. If a driver cannot drive, at any time, he is to contact the Bus Director. A driver is never to find his own substitute.

31. Talking while driving should be kept to an absolute minimum. Do not use this time to socialize with the workers or riders. Allow nothing to distract you from your driving. Conversations should be limited to that which is pertinent to the operation of the route.

Mr. Bus Driver,

May I remind you that what you are doing is unto the Lord — without you the buses cannot run.

POLICY INSTRUCTION

Subject:

The Bus Workers

1. The bus worker is a vital part of our Bus Program.

2. The Bus Worker position falls under the general responsibility of the Bus Captain of the route on which he is working.

3. He is to assist the Bus Captain in any way possible.

4. He is required to attend the Saturday, 9:30 a.m. meetings.

5. He is required to attend all the public meetings of our church, including Sunday school, morning and evening services and the midweek service. Attendance at special meetings, revivals, etc. is also required. "Moreover it is required in stewards that a man be found faithful" I Corinthians 4:2.

6. Helpers are to abide by the acceptable dress code of our bus ministry. Guys wear dress slacks and sport shirts; ties encouraged on Sundays. Girls wear dresses which are modest in skirt length and neck line. Slacks and shorts, etc. are never acceptable apparel.

POLICY INSTRUCTION

Subject:

The Bus Secretary

Remember that records enable us to follow-up and keep those who do come to our Sunday school. Yours is a very important facet of the team in operation.

1. The position of Bus Secretary falls under the general responsibility of the Bus Captain for that given route.

2. The main responsibility of the Bus Secretary is to keep the bus records of their route very much up-to-date.

3. The triplicate forms are to be used, and completed for each rider as they are enlisted on Saturday.

4. The records should be placed in the same order as the riders will be picked up on Sunday morning.

5. Use the triplicate forms in this manner:

A. Fill out the form completely.

B. When the new rider boards the bus on Sunday they should be given the yellow slip. They should be instructed to present it to their Sunday school class teacher.

C. The blue-green copy goes to the Bus Director as you check in each week.

D. The card-stock copy is retained by you. Attendance should be taken on your route each week.

6. Make a head count of each rider after the last rider has been picked up and before the bus arrives at the church.

7. Report in each Sunday by completing the form Bus Ministry Weekly Report found in the Sunday school office.

8. Make a head count after church, before the bus leaves the lot to return the riders.

9. Bus secretaries are required to visit a minimum of three hours per week.

10. Bus secretaries are required to attend the 9:30 a.m. Saturday bus meeting.

11. Bus secretaries are required to attend all the public services of our church including Sunday school, morning and evening services and the midweek services. Also attendance at special meetings, such as revivals, etc. is required. "Moreover it is required in stewards (secretaries) that a man be found faithful" I Corinthians 4:2.

12. Assist the Bus Captain in any way possible.

13. Secretaries are to wear modest apparel at all times. Slacks or shorts etc. are never acceptable clothing. Dresses should be of modest length and neckline, in accordance with the standards of a Christian lady and of our church.

14. Help keep discipline on the bus.

POLICY INSTRUCTION

Subject:

The Director of Bus Maintenance

Yours is a very important and essential part of the bus ministry. Without you our bus will not run.

1. The position of the Director of Bus Maintenance falls under the general responsibility of the Bus Director.

2. Supervise the maintenance and upkeep of all buses.

3. Make all decisions concerning matters of maintenance and upkeep.

4. Exercise great discretion in the expenditure of funds in keeping with the overall financial needs of our entire church work.

5. Consult with the Bus Director about any matters that you think may be pertinent.

6. Make sure all buses are maintained in a safe operating condition.

   A. All lights must work properly, especially head lights, tail lights, brake lights and turn signals.

B. All hand brakes must work.

C. All horns must work.

D. The back doors of each bus must be in working condition.

7. See that the buses are kept clean and attractive inside and outside.

8. Consult with the driver about minor and routine matters.

9. Arrange with the driver for his cooperation in the performance of minor and fairly routine maintenance.

10. Exert every possible and practical effort to insure that every bus is ready for operation every Sunday.

11. Arrange for each newly purchased bus to be ready for operation as rapidly as practical. Have the name of the church and the number of the bus painted on the bus before the first Sunday in operation, if at all possible.

12. Keep an extra key for each bus in a readily accessible place at all times.

13. Drive each bus as often as monthly, if possible, for a personal evaluation of the condition of the bus.

14. See that all maintenance is done from a Bus Work Sheet.

15. List all work completed on the Bus Work Sheet with a list of the cost on each job.

16. Each bus is to be filled with gas on Saturday, even if it will take only a small amount.

17. Assist the drivers in any way possible.

Hugh Ceruttic Shares Helpful Hints On Buying Buses

1. Some independent bus contractors will have buses for sale at the end of the school year.

2. Schools sometimes have buses for sale at the end of the school year on a bid basis.

3. Check the yellow pages in nearby cities for bus dealers. Most of these will have a supply of used buses on hand.

4. Check with your District Sunday School Director.

5. Ask churches in your area that have a bus ministry.
   a. Sometimes they have buses for sale.
   b. They usually keep some buses spotted all the time.
   c. They would know the best places to buy in your area.

6. It is best to stay with Fords, Chevrolets, GMC's or Internationals.
   a. Parts for these may be purchased in a salvage yard.
   b. A car engine will fit many of these with little modification.

7. Avoid "off brand" buses, rear engine units, and diesel buses.

8. Buy as large a bus as you can safely and conveniently turn in the area where it will be driven.

a. Consider where the bus will be operated, e.g., subdivision, housing area, etc.

b. Remember that it costs very little more to operate a 66 passenger bus than it would a 36 passenger.

9. School systems usually retire their buses when they are about 10 years old. These usually make the best buys.

a. They usually have been well maintained and kept in mechanical shape.

b. They sell from $1,000 to $2,000 in the midwest.

c. With proper maintenance a 10-year-old bus will run several years.

d. Remember you will not be driving them a great number of miles a year.

10. To determine the value of a particular bus determine what it would be worth if in good shape and then deduct any repairs that are needed. If possible have a mechanic check the condition of the following:

motor
brakes
transmission
rear end (differential)

Also check:
floor (this is a $300 item)
glass (deduct for any windows that must be

replaced)
body condition (are there badly rusted places?)
tires (these must be considered in the purchase price)

11. Ask other pastors who are involved in busing what a proper price for a particular age and make of bus should be. Also check several dealers to compare prices.

12. It is best to find a bus that ran last year on a school route.

a. Most of these have to meet certain standards and pass regular inspections.
b. Be aware, however, that items which schools are not forced to maintain they usually let go on a bus which they plan to trade.

13. Remember that the condition of the body is more important than the motor and transmission since these can be replaced much easier and at much less cost.

a. Check for rust around the doors and under the front fenders.
b. Galvanized bodies are rust resistant and usually built better.
c. Examine the seats—they cost about $10 each to recover.
d. Inspect the steering and front suspension.
e. Painting is easier if the present paint is in good shape.

14. Keep your buses in good maintenance. Pre-

vention is much cheaper than repairs.

a. Check the buses weekly—preferably on Saturday or early Sunday morning before they are taken on the routes.

b. Leaking water hoses can cause a major breakdown.

c. Likewise a broken or loose fan belt.

d. An oil leak can ruin the motor.

e. Safety features must be in good working order.

f. Serious defects should be reported and corrected before the bus is used.

15. Purchase major items needed for repair from a salvage yard.

16. Wholesale prices can usually be obtained on new parts if you explain that you have a fleet of buses or that they are owned by a church.

Hugh Ceruttic Shares Helpful Hints On The Weekly Church Bus Check-Up

Listed below are duties each driver should do before starting his run.

1. Check engine oil level and gasoline gauge.

2. Check radiator collant level.

3. Check fan belt tension.

4. Make sure ignition wires are in place.

5. Make sure the hood is securely fastened.

6. Look under the bus for oil or coolant leaks.

7. Check tires to be sure they are properly inflated and wheel lugs are secure.

8. Clean lights, windows, mirrors, signs, license plates, and reflectors.

9. Clean floor and seats.

10. See that the emergency door is securely closed and entrance door works.

11. Remove all obstacles from entrance step or in driver's compartments.

12. Determine that all emergency equipment is

available and operating: fire extinguisher, first aid kits, fuses, reflectors and flags.

13. Be sure there are no obstacles in bus aisle.

14. Start motor for warm-up.

15. Check horn, windshield wiper, heater and defroster.

16. Read all dashboard gauges.

17. Check steering.

18. Test brakes.

19. Report any defects.

Always practice safety first. A few moments spent on checking is easier made up in the parking area than in the cemetary.

TRIPLICATE BUS FORM

1. The triplicate form is the best provided for maintaining records on the individual bus rider.

a. They fit on an arch board (obtainable at nearly any stationery or office supply store) giving the bus captain a handy, permanent, and durable record of each rider. There is space to record the attendance of each rider for one year.

b. For a first time rider, copy A is given to him to take with him to class. It is given to the teacher and serves as a quick and accurate introduction to the student.

c. Copy B is given to the general secretary of the Sunday school. It contains all the information needed to enroll the new pupil.

d. Copy C (card stock) is retained by the bus captain and placed on his arch board. It provides a one year record system on each pupil and can be carried on his Saturday visitation. It also serves as a guide to an assistant or substitute driver on Sunday morning.

The arch board and individual record cards should be guarded against loss or destruction. They are valuable!

2. A permanent file of bus riders should be maintained by the Sunday school general secretary or

a special secretary of busing. Form A (illustrated below) is a suggested enrollment form.

FORM "A"

Name:____________________Phone:__________
Address:__________________________________
City:_____Zip:_____Age:___Birthday:________
Parent's Name:_____________________________
Remarks:__________________________________
____
Route:___________Captain:__________________

3. Form B is filled out by each bus pastor or captain and turned in to the director of bus ministry each Sunday. These are filed for a permanent record. They also serve as a report of the bus captain's visitation.

FORM "B" INDIVIDUAL BUS RECORD

Today's Date______Rt. No.__________________
Number of Riders___________________________
Number of First-Timers______________________
Day(s) You Visited_________________________
Hours You Visited__________________________
Number of Workers Who Visited____________
Departure Time____________________________
Arrival Time_______________________________
Was Your Driver on Time?_________________
List Wkrs. & Hrs. Vis. on Back
Signature__________________________________

REPAIR SHEET

BUS REPAIR
& COMMENT SHEET

DATE ________

Repairs Needed: ________________________________
____
____
____

- -

General Comments: ______________________________
____
____
____

Bus Route & No. ________________________________

Driver: ________________

FORM "E"

Bus Maintenance

Date ______________________________ Bus Route & No. ______________

Date	Description of Work Completed	Mechanic	Cost	Gas	Oil	Mileage

FORM "C"

Bus Ministry Weekly Report

Date ______________________________

Rt. No.	NAME	Departure Time	Arrival Time	Hours Visited	1st Time Visitors	Total Riders
	TOTAL					

Checked By: ______________________________

NOTES

NOTES

NOTES

NOTES

NOTES

NOTES